The

GIRLBOSS

Workbook

Other books by Sophia Amoruso

#GIRLBOSS

Nasty Galaxy

The

GIRLBOSS

Workbook

An Interactive Journal for Winning at Life

Sophia Amoruso

Illustrated by Grace Danico

Cover art by Galen Pehrson

Portfolio / Penguin
G. P. Putnam's Sons
New York

Portfolio/Penguin
G. P. Putnam's Sons

Imprints of Penguin Random House LLC
375 Hudson Street
New York, New York 10014

Most Portfolio books are available at a discount when purchased in quantity
for sales promotions or corporate use. Special editions, which include personalized
covers, excerpts, and corporate imprints, can be created when purchased in
large quantities. For more information, please call (212) 572-2232 or e-mail
specialmarkets@penguinrandomhouse.com. Your local bookstore can also assist
with discounted bulk purchases using the Penguin Random House corporate
Business-to-Business program. For assistance in locating a participating retailer,
e-mail B2B@penguinrandomhouse.com.

Library of Congress Cataloging-in-Publication Data

Names: Amoruso, Sophia, author.
Title: The girlboss workbook : an interactive journal for winning at life /
Sophia Amoruso ; illustrated by Grace Danico.
Description: New York : Portfolio/Penguin/G. P. Putnam's Sons, [2017]
Identifiers: LCCN 2017027147 | ISBN 9780143131977 (pbk.)
Subjects: LCSH: Businesswomen. | Success in business. | Success. |
Motivation (Psychology)
Classification: LCC HD6053 .A563 2017 | DDC 650.1—dc23 LC record
available at https://lccn.loc.gov/2017027147

Printed in the United States of America
1   3   5   7   9   10   8   6   4   2

Illustrations by Grace Danico

This book is for all the poodles.

The
GIRLBOSS

Oath

I will live deliberately. I will work with intention, play with intention, and love with intention. I will take nothing at face value, ask questions, and write my own rules. I will wake up every day to fight the most important battle of my life: my life. I will be curious and trust that, in time, my questions will answer themselves. I will play to my strengths, sniff out my shortcomings, and stomp out ego at every opportunity. I will take my life seriously without taking myself seriously. I will fight for what I believe, burn my armchair, and remember that success is something that only I define for myself.

front

(cut)
↓

GIRLBOSS

NAME

_____

IDGAF QUOTE

_____

Draw a
Selfie

back

(cont)
↓

MEMBERSHIP CARD

MEMBER SINCE

_____

SIGNED

_____

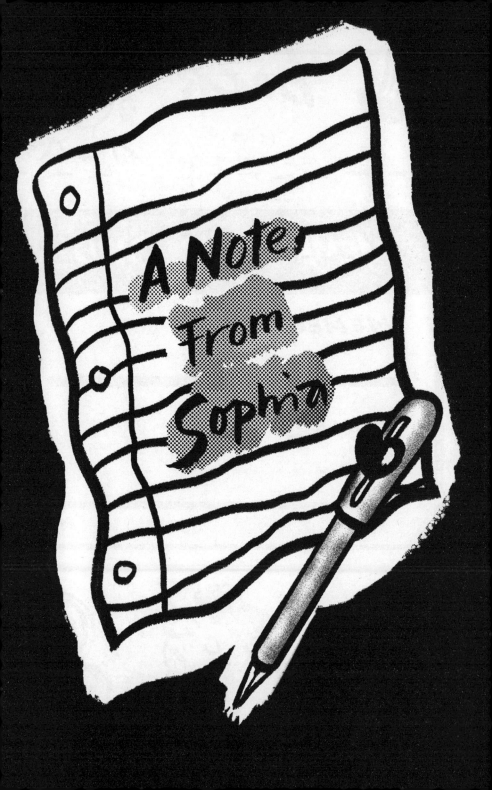

Use this book and use
it again. Since I wrote
#GIRLBOSS four years ago,
I've had some hard-won wins
and some very public stumbles.
With *The Girlboss Workbook*,
I'm bringing you everything
I know and serving up some
wisdom filets, medium rare.
Hijack your life beyond your
wildest dreams and remember
that action is the breeding
ground of serendipity. Turn
the page; change your life.
And most of all, have some
fun along the way.

XO,
Sophia

DREAM

CAREERS

_____

_____

_____

_____

_____

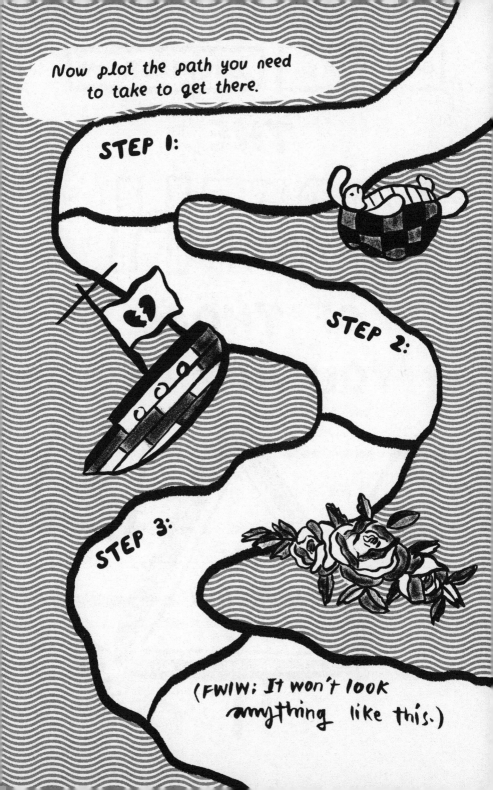

← REVERSE ENGINEER →

THE PATH

OF THOSE YOU ADMIRE.

USE LINKEDIN

NAME/JOB:

_____

PREVIOUS JOB: RELEVANT SKILLS:

_____   _____

JOB BEFORE THAT: RELEVANT SKILLS:

_____   _____

FIRST JOB: RELEVANT SKILLS:

_____   _____

DETOURS:

_____

———————————————————————————————————————

NAME/JOB:

_____

PREVIOUS JOB: RELEVANT SKILLS:

_____   _____

JOB BEFORE THAT: RELEVANT SKILLS:

_____   _____

FIRST JOB: RELEVANT SKILLS:

_____   _____

DETOURS:

_____

———————————————————————————————————————

NAME/JOB:

_____

PREVIOUS JOB: RELEVANT SKILLS:

_____   _____

JOB BEFORE THAT: RELEVANT SKILLS:

_____   _____

FIRST JOB: RELEVANT SKILLS:

_____   _____

DETOURS:

_____

- [ ] My product or service is differentiated and truly stands out from the mush.

- [ ] My product or service can improve the lives of a big-ass audience.

- [ ] I can explain what my brand is in a single sentence.

- [ ] People will recognize my brand when they see it.

- [ ] My brand is beautiful, visually compelling, and shareable on social media.

- [ ] No, scratch that—it's *brag worthy.*

MY THREE BHAGS

BIG,

HAIRY,

AUDACIOUS

GOALS

_____

_____

_____

BUSINESS BUILDING CHECKLIST

☐ I can monetize my brand—either through selling a product, service, or my audience.

☐ My business has a bulletproof reason to exist and is solving a real problem in the marketplace.

☐ I have identified my own weaknesses, the weaknesses of the business, and many potential pitfalls. (Bonus: I have some ideas about how to circumvent them.)

☐ I know what I want to build—and have worked backward to create actionable steps that will get me there.

☐ I've opened a bank account for the company.

☐ I've registered as an LLC or corporation, to protect myself.

☐ I made some bangin' business cards.

Three SKILLS to LEARN

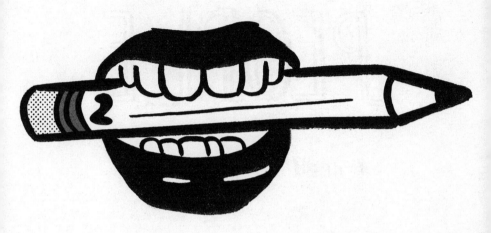

Five PEOPLE

I need to meet . . .

_____

_____

_____

_____

_____

and the five people
who might be able to
introduce me.

THE BASIC ETIQUETTE OF NETWORKING

1. Ask for an introduction from a mutual friend and be clear with your intentions.

2. In your email, include any relevant links that help illustrate who you are and why you'd love to meet.

3. Find a common thread.

4. Make it easy on them: Ask for a five-minute phone call or a ten-minute coffee adjacent to their office.

5. If they agree to meet IRL, pay the bill as a thank-you for their time.

BUFF THAT LINKEDIN PROFILE

- [ ] Your photo is high quality and straightforward, that is, not from da club, da beach, or a college formal. Don't pick a photo where your eyes are obscured or you have to crop out a date, friend, or dog.

- [ ] You've included some details about each role, not just your title.

- [ ] You've tested all outbound links to ensure they're valid.

- [ ] You are using a personal email address.

- [ ] You're following relevant brands and influencers that ideally make you look smart.

- [ ] You've cut all grandiose, eye-rolling language—in other words, don't refer to yourself as a visionary, thought leader, or trailblazer.

- [ ] You've acknowledged unemployment gaps honestly—don't call yourself a consultant or freelancer unless it's real.

Last Ditch Checklist

- ☐ My résumé is organized, well designed, and in a legibly sized font.

- ☐ My contact information is provided.

- ☐ All gaps in unemployment are explained.

- ☐ Extraneous information has been sliced and diced.

- ☐ I checked my righting and grammer and its purrfect.

THE COVER LETTER Recipe

MY COVER LETTER IS . . .

- [ ] Brief—my résumé does the talking.

- [ ] Specific—I cared enough to do my research.

- [ ] Appealing—I've done my research and know how to articulate my value to the hiring manager.

HERE, I DID THE WORK FOR YOU!

Dear _____ (name of hiring manager),

I am writing in regard to the opening for _____ (name of position). I have been admiring _____ (name of company) for ___ (years/months), ever since _____ (flex your powers of observation here). I love that you are _____ (pioneering/taking the lead/so thoughtful about/focused on) _____ (audience/segment/product) because _____ (it resonates with me/resonates with the culture/resonates with what the world needs/is F-ing cool).

I'm sure you've been overwhelmed with candidates, but I am throwing my hat in the ring because I would love to _____ (contribute to/participate in/help power) what you are building. I am currently _____ (position/company), where I _____ (skills/progress you've made/work hard). If it seems like an appropriate fit, I would love the opportunity to interview; if you're looking for a different profile, I would so appreciate your keeping my résumé on file in the event another position becomes available.

Best,

_____

(P.S. I did not completely lift my cover letter from The Girlboss Workbook and instead made it my own.)

- Have the right skills. If not, offer ways in which you intend to bridge the gap (for example, you are taking HTML classes at General Assembly or learning Photoshop through lynda.com).

- Come prepared with good, well-researched questions about the company and culture.

- Come physically prepared with a printed résumé and a physical portfolio (if relevant).

- Listen carefully and answer the actual questions.

- Be open, honest, and candid—yet diplomatic.

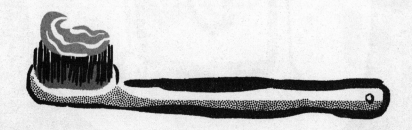

- Are you unable to justify your string of short-term jobs?

- Are you a bummer and hard to talk to?

- Are you eager to talk shit about previous employers or coworkers?

- Do you hoard ideas, inflate your own experience, or take credit for the work of others in your résumé or portfolio?

- Were you late to the interview?

- Did you wear flip-flops, lingerie, butt-grazing skirts, shorts, or athletic wear?

- Did you seem overly interested in hours required and extra perks?

ON LANDING THE ROLE

- Don't play hard to get—this isn't a date.

- If you don't feel particularly excited, fake it!

- If you are particularly excited, show it—but don't be desperate.

- Apply through the supplied HR link, but then sleuth around to figure out who the hiring manager may be and reach out directly.

- Be patient—silence doesn't mean that it's over.

- Follow up in due time. Send that thank-you note, then wait a beat. After enough time has passed, be brave and ask if they've filled the position.

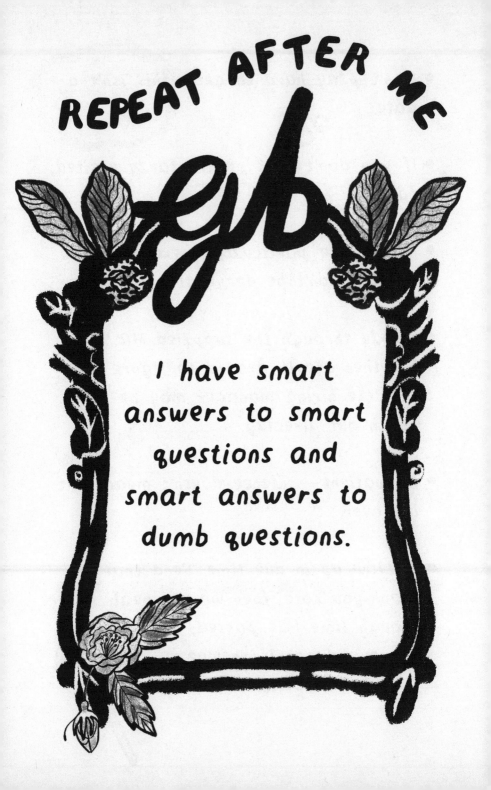

THREE QUESTIONS FOR MY INTERVIEW

_____

_____

_____

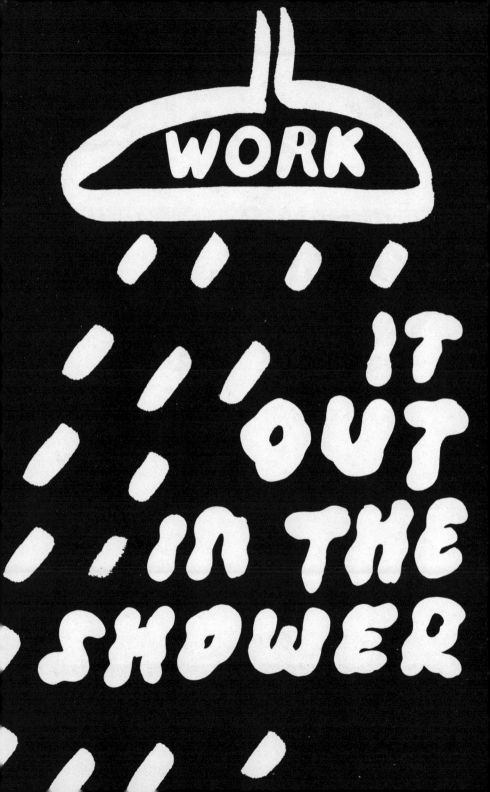

What are your strengths? Weaknesses? What's your relevant experience? Career history? Work out the questions you want to be prepared to answer—and then practice.

Do your Research, GINA

MAKE A LIST OF FACTS ABOUT THE COMPANY THAT WOULD BE GOOD TO KNOW AHEAD OF TIME.

Founder's Name:

Founder's Story:

Founded In:

General Path/Trajectory:

Key Products:

# of Employees:

# of Offices:

Expressed Path Forward:

Relevant Press:

Hiring Manager's Role:

Hiring Manager's Career Trajectory/History:

THE

Thank
Yon

EMAIL

Dear _____ (hiring manager),

Thank you so much for meeting with me _____ (yesterday/Tuesday/last week). I really appreciate that you took so much time to discuss the role, and whether my experience might be the right fit. I _____ (something awesome that you observed/something that they shared). I wanted to reiterate that I would love to do a _____ (project/memo) to illustrate how I would approach the role. I hope to hear from you soon!

All my best,

_____

What have you done at work that is "not your job"?

What more can you do that is not your job that would help your company? Make a list!

Some
May
Come
some may
GO

READY TO PEACE OUT ON YOUR CURRENT JOB?

Ask for five minutes, thank your manager profusely for the opportunity, and give at least two full weeks' notice. Take a beat before starting the new job—you need to recharge!

THINGS TO ACCOMPLISH IN MY DOWNTIME BETWEEN JOBS:

HEY THERE:

DON'T BE A

Toxic

COWORKER

QUEEN OF THE WATERCOOLER? These are your coworkers, not your college besties—if you spend more time socializing than working, sit your ass down because everyone has already noticed.

ARE YOU THE SOURCE? It's hard to resist office gossip, but if you find that you are becoming everyone's go-to for dirt, reassess.

DO PEOPLE AVOID PARTNERING WITH YOU? From afar, it can be easy to spot lone sheep, that is, people who refuse to collaborate. If this is you, ask for some mentoring and be open to some coaching.

ARE YOU CONSISTENTLY OVERLOOKED FOR GOOD ASSIGNMENTS? Something is wrong. Have the hard conversation with your boss and actively look for ways to improve.

ARE YOU RESISTANT? Change is hard. If you find yourself saying "no" more than "let's find a way," you're clogging up the company's progress.

Plan your mini pity party, throw it, and have a great time.

Then **look for the lesson** and move on!

Don't
DO
THIS
EVEN IF IT
WOULD
FEEL good

CALL ANYONE A BITCH, C-WORD, OR ASSHOLE. *(That's verbal abuse.)*

RALLY YOUR FORMER COWORKERS. *(I know you're hurting, but that's childish.)*

COMPLAIN ON THE INTERNET. *(It might feel cathartic in the moment, but it's not so smart in the long run.)*

USE THE FIRING MANAGER AS A REFERENCE. *(Obvious, yes, but apparently not obvious enough.)*

MAKE A SCENE ON THE WAY OUT. *(They will call security.)*

HAVE YOUR PARENTS CALL. *(It happens.)*

SO YOU DIDN'T GET THE JOB

REPEAT AFTER ME:
"It's not personal."
"Everything happens for a reason."
"Onward!"

SHAKE IT OFF, GET BACK ON THE JOB BOARDS, AND MAKE A LIST OF OPEN POSITIONS BELOW.

Company	Open Position	Applied

DEBT is a SHIT-ANCHOR

Before you can help yourself, pay down your debts and at minimum get up to speed on monthly payments.

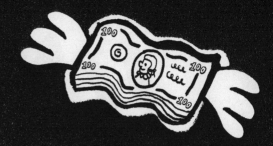

THE THINGS I'LL CHANGE TO BECOME DEBT FREE

_____

_____

_____

TIME SPENT
making
MONEY
100
100
100
100
GREATER THAN
TIME SPENT SPENDING MONEY

Fill in a pie chart that represents the current ratio of your time spent.

Fill in your goal pie chart here:

MONTHLY TAKE-HOME PAY (POST-TAXES): _____

10% OF MY PAY TO SAVE: _____

MONTHLY EXPENSES (TOTAL): _____

COLLEGE LOANS: _____

CREDIT CARD PAYMENT: _____

RENT/MORTGAGE: _____

CHILDCARE: _____

UTILITIES: _____

INTERNET/CABLE: _____

PHONE: _____

HEALTHCARE: _____

CAR PAYMENT: _____

GAS: _____

GROCERIES: _____

RESTAURANTS: _____

BARS: _____

COFFEE SHOPS: _____

CLOTHING: _____

ENTERTAINMENT: _____

TRAVEL: _____

INCIDENTALS: _____

NONPROFIT DONATIONS: _____

OTHER: _____

WHAT'S LEFT FOR FUN AFTER ALL OF THAT:

_____

SUPER BASIC LIFE CALCULATOR

How much I make every month:
      Subtracted by

How much I spend every month:
      Equals

How much is left over at the end of the month:

      and

The percentage I will commit to saving (circle one):
5%   10%   15%   20%   30%

Multiplied by 12 equals

How much I'll save by the end of this year as a result:

            Hint: Try the 50/20/30 rule.
            50% of your income should go toward
            essential costs (fixed expenses).

            30% should be allocated to lifestyle
            choices (variable expenses).

            20% should go toward financial
            priorities, like paying off debt or
            growing your savings account.

Open a savings account, set up autopay from your checking account in the amount of 10 percent of your salary, and lose the password. Wake up next year with thousands of dollars in the bank.

HOW TO Haggle for VINTAGE

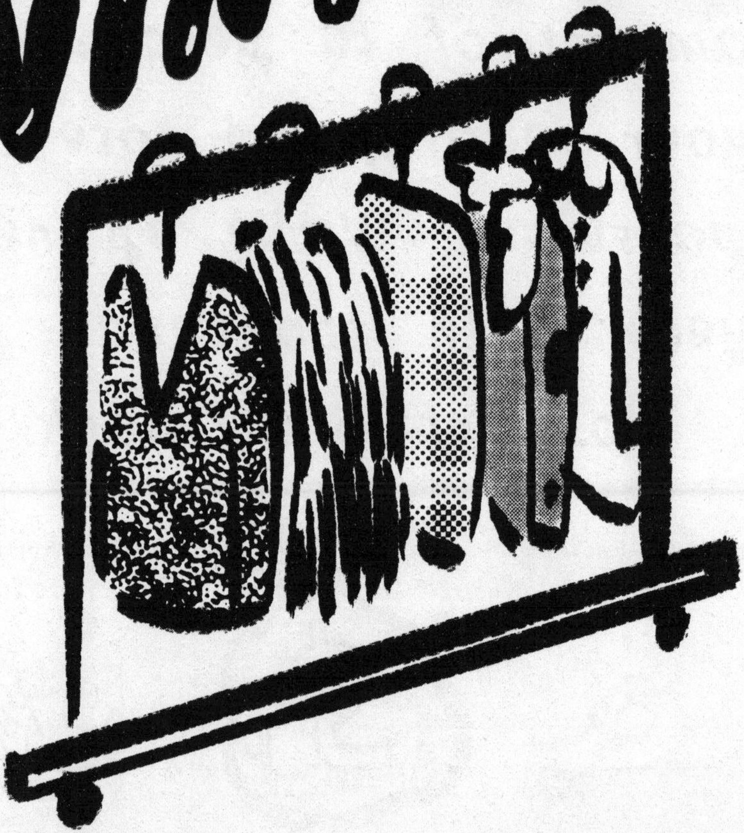

1. You blow it the second you drive up in an expensive car, so just don't.

2. It's easier to negotiate for things other people don't want.

3. Have cash on hand in case you're dealing with someone who wants to be paid under the table.

4. Bundle, bundle, bundle!

5. Go so low you insult them a little, but never a lot.

6. Leverage is everything: Are there other opportunities waiting in the wings? On the flip side, can you offer things in addition to cash? (No blow jobs or family heirlooms.)

7. Comparison shop.

8. Be willing to walk away.

9. If you aren't in a position to walk away, try the above, and if you fail, agree to their terms and, for Christ's sake, withhold the tears until you are alone.

HOW TO KEEP FROM GOING BANKRUPT!

1. Have minimal debt.

2. Hire just enough people (that is, not too many).

3. Don't plan for growth that you have no idea how to get.

4. Avoid investors if you can.

5. Grow reasonably—don't try to grow too fast.

6. Don't try to do too many things at once.

7. Focus your business.

8. When people start copying you, evolve.

9. Know that no deal is done until the paper is signed and the money wired.

10. Understand that Hail Marys almost never, ever materialize.

11. Never take any risks, ever. Just kidding.

ORGANIZE A STRIKE AMONG YOUR FRIENDS. STRIKE ALCOHOL. STRIKE LAZINESS. STRIKE BOREDOM. FILL IN THE SIGN BELOW ACCORDINGLY.

DEFACE THIS WORD WITH YOUR BEST GRAFFITI.

CITIES TO VISIT BEFORE I DIE

_____
_____
_____
_____
_____
_____
_____
_____
_____
_____

WRITE A KIND NOTE BELOW, TEAR IT OUT, AND LEAVE IT ON SOMEONE'S WINDSHIELD. MAKE THEIR DAY.

Other ways I can pay it forward

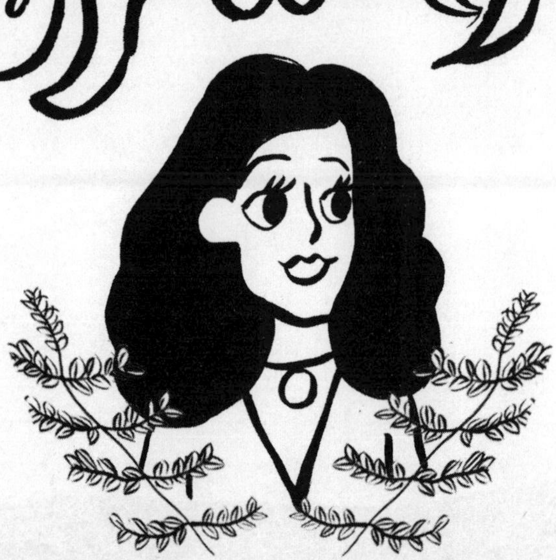

Draw a picture of YOURSELF.

Put on your BEST lipstick

AND COVER THE PAGE IN KISSES.

SELF(IE)-LOVE!

DELETE ALL
SOCIAL MEDIA
APPS FOR A WEEK.
GET YOUR

BACK.

NOW

Take

A

Deeeeeeeep

BREATH

___
___

THE LIFE-CHANGING MAGIC OF TIDYING UP YOUR RELATIONSHIPS

Who was there for you the last time the shit hit the fan? Who *wasn't* there for you? Keep the former, lose the latter. Life's too short and you're about to get *real* busy.

RIDE or DIE Friends

_____
_____
_____
_____
_____
_____
_____
_____
_____

FAIR Weather Friends

_____
_____
_____
_____
_____
_____
_____
_____

Now rip them out of this book like you'll
rip them out of your life.

PROFESSIONALIZE

your Self-Care

You put meetings on the calendar, so why not put the things that benefit you personally on one as well? Hold yourself accountable to that bubble bath, Pilates class, meditation, and sleep!

BANDS TO SEE LIVE BEFORE I DIE

IF YOU WERE A COMBINATION OF FOUR BADASS WOMEN, WHO WOULD THEY BE? DRAW THEM HERE.

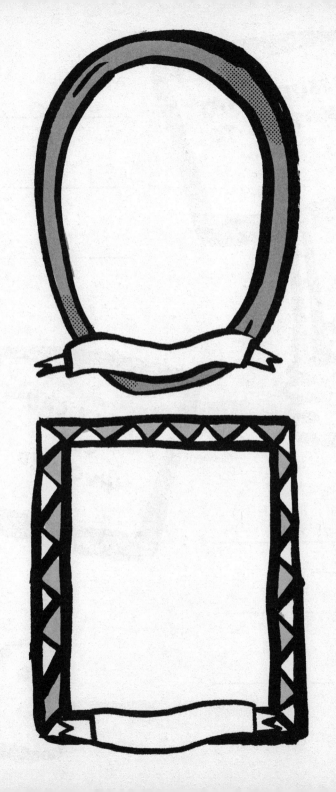

PROTEST PACKING LIST

- Comfortable shoes

- Plenty of layers (long-sleeve tops you can tie around your waist)

- Sunscreen, hat, water, and snacks!

- A badass sign

- A spare phone charger

- $20 bills, contact info for your friends in case your phone dies, and a printed meet-up plan and map in case you can't get a signal

- Bandana in case shit gets real

LIFE is a MARATHON, not a RACE

WHAT DO YOU WANT TO HAPPEN RIGHT NOW? PLOT IT OUT ON A FIVE-YEAR PLAN. REMEMBER, THE BEST THINGS TAKE TIME.

What I want now:

In four years, I'll need to:

In three years, I'll need to:

In two years, I'll need to:

This year, I must begin:

Invent a BEAUTIFUL Lie about yourself

How you'll make it come TRUE

CALL

Someone

AND TELL

Them

YOU Love THEM

Plan your words here.

TODAY, COMPLIMENT THREE STRANGERS AND REALLY MEAN IT.

KIDNAP A FRIEND AND MAKE HER HAPPY!
Itinerary of Her Perfect Day

Breakfast:

Mid-Morning Interlude:

Lunch:

Afternoon Activity:

Dinner:

Post 9 p.m.:

DESIGN A
TROPHY
FOR
YOUR
FUTURE

MY TROPHY

Now go win it.

My

LEMONADE

Recipe

The lemons: _____
(That is, what is sucking right now?)

The Sugar: _____
(What's the bright side? And what can I
learn from this?)

Here's the lemonade: _____
(What I learned.)

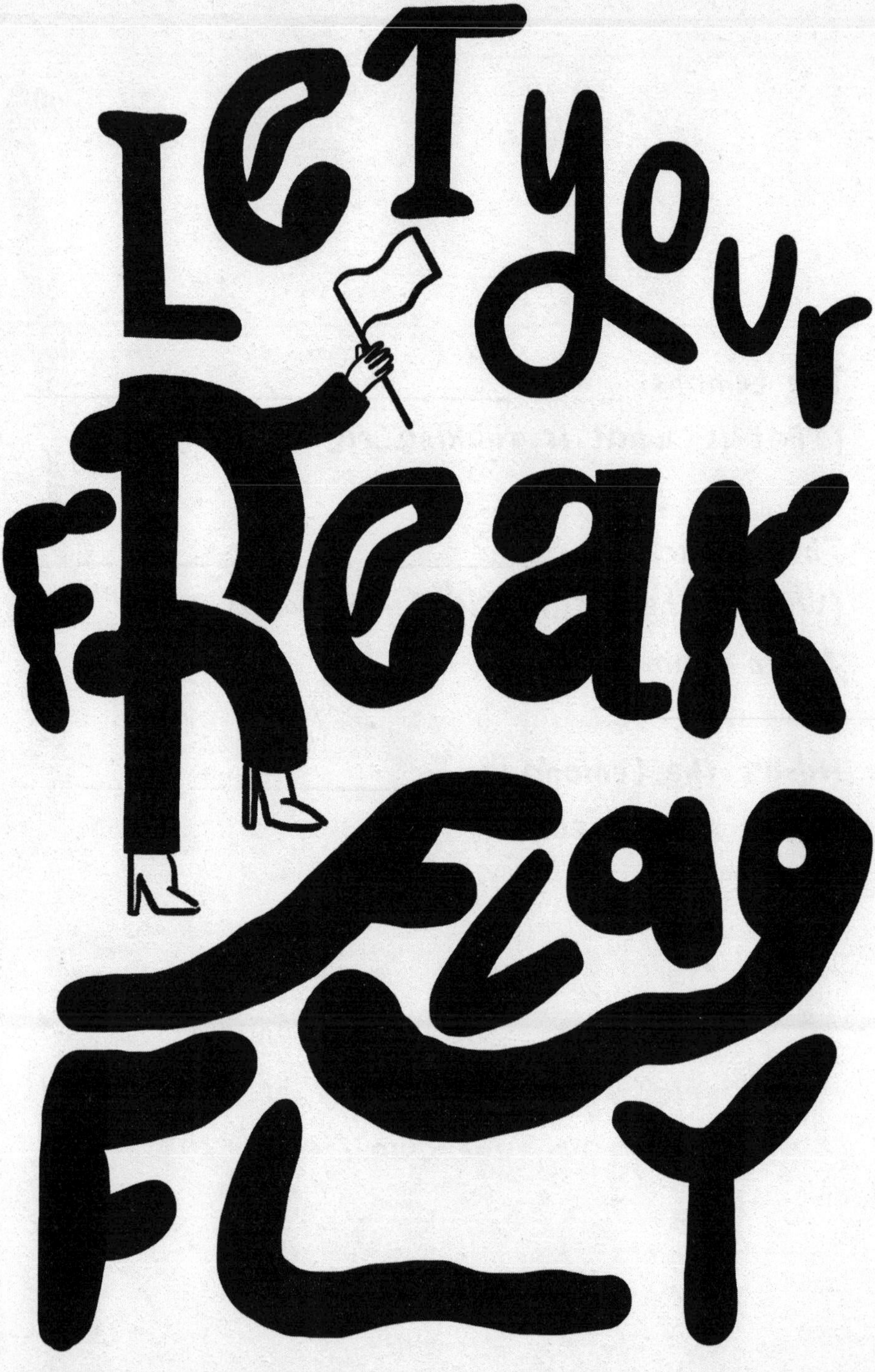
LET YOUR FREAK FLAG FLY

What does yours look like?
Which colors and why? Symbol? Basic?
Fabric? Pleather? Big? Subtle? Go wild!
Draw your own freak flag.

TIPS FOR MOIST

WAYS I SHOW SELF-LOVE

AGING WELL

URIZE

Chug an entire glass of water right now. Refill it and keep it next to you as you continue to turn the pages . . .

IT'S OK TO FAIL

Write down the last time you failed
and what you learned from it.

Now spin it into gold

CONGRATS, RUMPELSTILTSKIN!

Sigil Magic

(Or How to Embed Your Conscious into Your Subconscious and Vice Versa)

Get a piece of paper and a pen.

1. Write a sentence describing your desire. "I happily own my own profitable small business."

2. Remove all of the vowels and duplicate letters in each word. HLYWNMYWNPRFTBLSMBSN.

3. Now reduce this to a symbol, chiseling away at its extraneous parts, and doodle until you are left with a symbol you are happy with.

4. Treasure it. Hang with it. Say your final good-byes.

5. Cast your sigil: Burn it while thinking diligently about what it is that you want.

6. Put your desires into action to help your sigil help you IRL.

7. I'll say it again: Action is the breeding ground of serendipity . . .

Replace all of your passwords with phrases that reflect your dreams, goals, and desires.

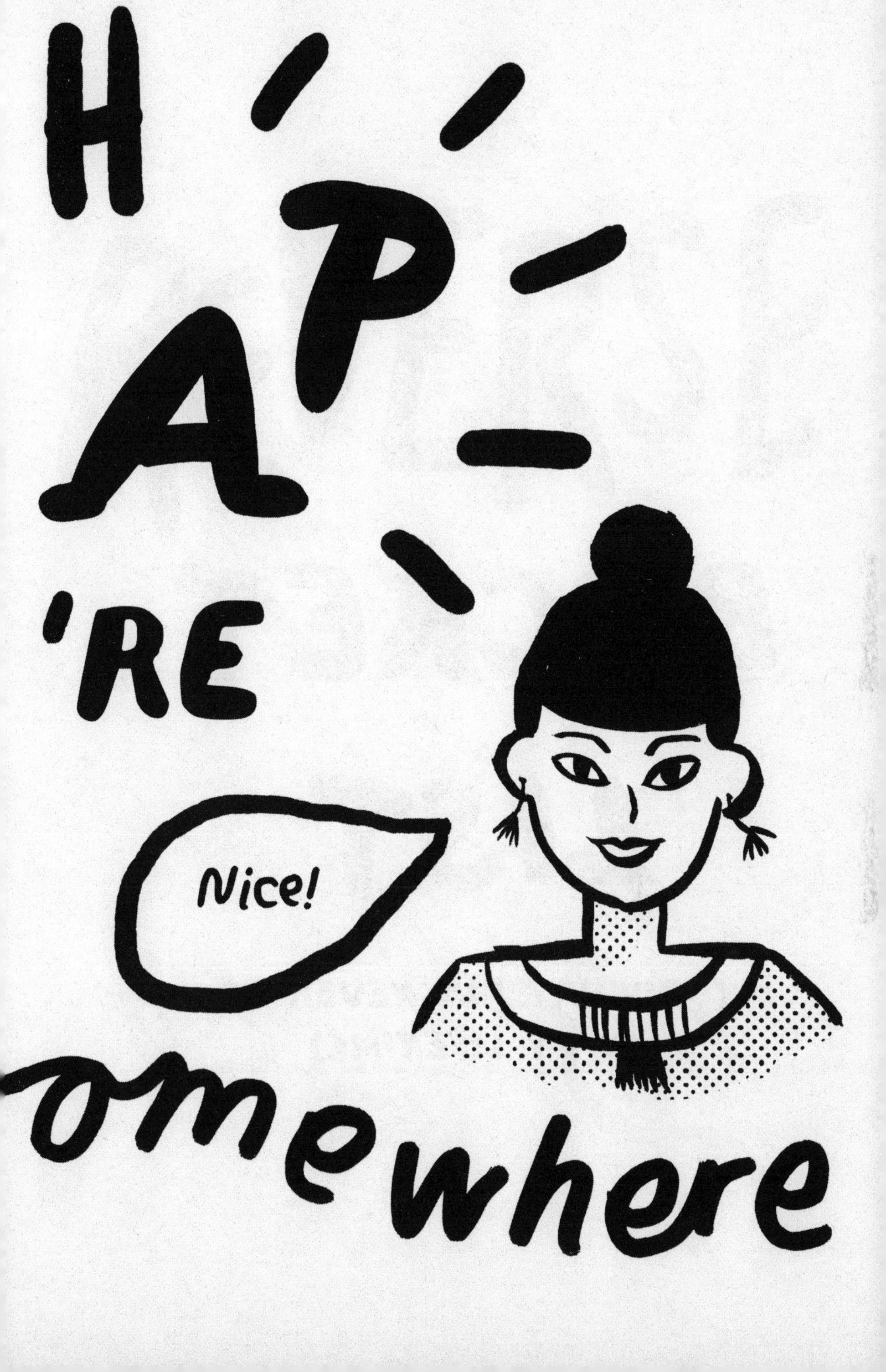
H
A P
'RE
Nice!
omewhere

REVERSE BUCKET LIST

BUCKET

LIST

(OR WHAT I'LL NEVER DO
IN MY LIFETIME)

1. Register to vote (absentee ballots are the most convenient).

2. Actually vote when it's time to.

3. Research issues that matter to you and sign up for digital newsletters that can keep you informed. Start with the *New York Times.*

4. Leave your filter bubble to understand how other people see the world. This builds empathy. Ever think about running for office? More women than ever are. Explain your platform here:

We all have some. Nobody's parents are perfect. The world isn't perfect either, and life is unfair. list your damage here.

_____

_____

_____

_____

_____

_____

NOW REPEAT AFTER ME:
"Nobody but me is going to turn my damage into opportunity. I refuse to excuse myself because of my damage. As an adult, I get to right all of the wrongs and heal my damage through action."

DON'T COMPARE YOUR HUSTLE TO THEIR HIGHLIGHT REEL—THEY'RE ALL FULL OF SHIT, ANYWAY.

PUTTING THE
ART IN
SANDWICH ARTIST

Remember, all actions are
creative: Turn what you don't
love doing into a game.
Compete with yourself. Convince
yourself that each time you do
something small, it's a prayer
for a future better than you
can even imagine today.

Things I Abhor Doing

Things I Can Do to Infuse Fun into My Routine

What Are the Weirdest Things About Me?

I'M PROUDA YOU. ARMPIT FARTS ALL AROUND.

How To DISARM Anyone

1. Be curious

2. Be a beginner: Ask questions

3. Be kind

4. Be self-deprecating

5. Be funny

6. Never take yourself too seriously

MY INSPIRING-ASS OBITUARY

_____ passed away on
_____ at the age of
_____. She was always
_____. She never
_____. When she entered a
room, _____, and she would
always say, _____, which
became her slogan. No one was quite as
_____ as she was. She was
known for _____ because
_____. Throughout her
career, she _____, and
piloted _____,
_____, and
_____. She is survived by
_____, _____,
and _____. Fun fact that she
never told anyone: _____.

FRANK ZAPPA SAID THE UGLIEST PART OF YOUR BODY IS YOUR MIND, AND HE MAY HAVE BEEN RIGHT.

Draw your favorite body part below.

FUCK YOUR IDOLS

Be your own hero. Draw yourself below.
Cape provided.

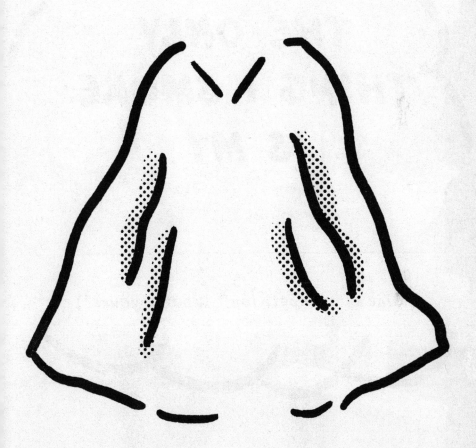

THE ONLY THING I SMOKE IS MY

_____.

(Mine's "competition." What's yours?)

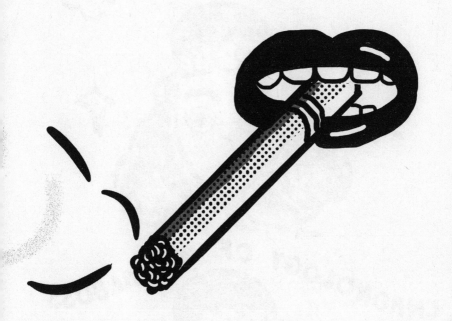

THE

CHRONOLOGY OF A GIRLBOSS

When I was five, I wiped poop on the preschool bathroom wall.

Chart your funniest and proudest moments below, along with your hopes, dreams, and battle plans for the future.

Age 0-10:

Age 10-15:

Age 15-20:

Age 20-25:

Age 25-30:

Age 30-35:

Age 35-40:

Age 40-50:

Age 50-60:

Age 60-70:

Age 70-80:

Age 80+:

HERE'S a PAPER airplane.

(YOU'RE WELCOME.)

Write your haters' names on it and throw it off the tallest thing you can find. BYEEEE, psychic garbage!

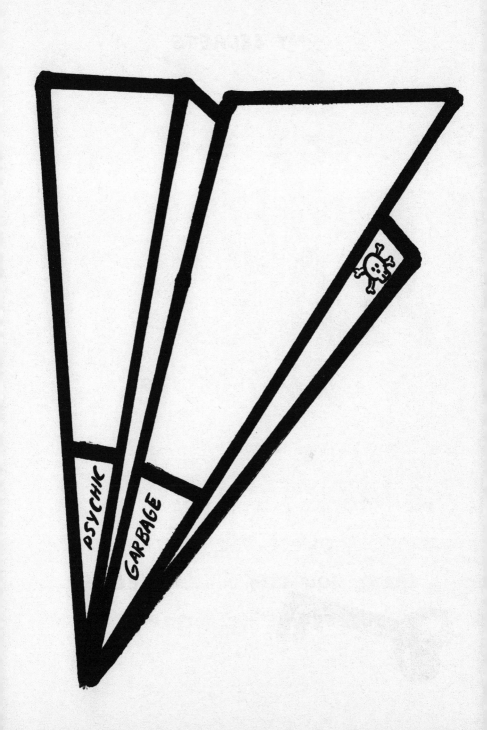

MY SECRETS

I fucked up _____,
I fucked up _____,
I fucked up _____,
I fucked up _____,
I fucked up _____,

LET'S CHART MORE OF THOSE FUCK UPS.

and I learned that _____

and I learned that _____

and I learned that _____

and I learned that _____

and I learned that _____

Tell them you're writing a big story on them and take them out to eat. Flattery goes a long way.

THINGS I'LL NEVER TOLERATE IN A ROMANTIC RELATIONSHIP

_____

_____

_____

_____

_____

_____

_____

_____

_____

_____

_____

_____

_____

_____

_____

_____

_____

PINKY

SWEAR

WITH YOURSELF

FIVE THINGS I WANT TO LEARN TO DO

1 _____

2 _____

3 _____

4 _____

5 _____

MY BIGGEST FEARS
Name them, claim them, and release them.
Now you have the power.

WRITE A PARAGRAPH ABOUT YOURSELF THAT YOU NEVER WANT TO BE UNTRUE.

_____

_____

_____

_____

_____

_____

_____

_____

_____

_____

_____

_____

_____

_____

_____

_____

_____

_____

_____

HOW TO HAVE A
⸗ GREAT ⸗
DATE

Do something you'd like to do anyway.

MY DREAM DATES

_____

_____

_____

_____

_____

_____

_____

_____

MENU

QUALITIES IN PARTNERS
I THINK I'M INTO
(circle your faves)

SIMPLE *Stylish* Relaxed TYPE A

CURIOUS

COMPLICATED SMART

STRONG

and SILENT

FUNNY MESSY

KINKY

Philantropic

COIFFED

TECHY GOOD WITH MONEY$ EXHIBITIONIST

PLANFUL GREEN THUMB

SPONTANEOUS GOOD WITH DIRECTIONS SELF AWARE MUSICAL

TRAVELER SNUGGLY HAIRY QUIET

Kind ENTITLED

Elegant Great Cook LOW KEY Snarky

AMBITIOUS GREGARIOUS ARTISTIC

Fart in bed

Poop with the door open

Complain constantly

Party all the time

Stop taking care of yourself

Forget birthdays and anniversaries

FAVORITE SONG LYRICS

MY *Perfect* WEEKEND

Something beautiful: _____

Something tasty: _____

Something scentual: _____

Something sensual: _____

Something big: _____

Something small: _____

Something near: _____

Something far: _____

Someone I like: _____

Someone I love: _____

Something I want: _____

Something I want to read: _____

My dream dream: _____

BOOKS I PROMISE TO READ

1.
2.
3.
4.
5.
6.
7.
8.
9.
10.

. . . AND I KEEP MY PROMISES

MY HANDBAG INVENTORY

Now throw half of it away.

MY BEST QUALITIES

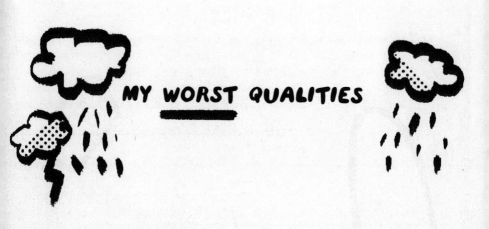

MY WORST QUALITIES

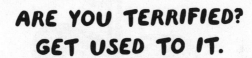

**ARE YOU TERRIFIED?
GET USED TO IT.**

*If what you're doing doesn't terrify you,
we have problems.*

ACKNOWLEDGMENTS

Thank you to Galen Pehrson, for your love, support, and for designing our gorgeous cover. To Grace Danico for illustrating her ass off. Thank you to Kerri Kolen, Andy McNicol, Gary Stiffelman, Elise Loehnen, Terry Bird, Maggie Renshaw, Ana Orrego, Donna, Cosi, Gino, my mother for reminding me to take my own advice, and my father for your tough love. Thank you also to team Girlboss: Neha Gandhi, Alison Wyatt, Jerico Mandybur, Deena Drewis, Tori Borengasser, Lindsey O'Hara, Chloe Parks, and Meghan Raab.

SOPHIA AMORUSO is the founder and CEO of Girlboss Media, a platform for women exploring success on their own terms through content, community, and shared experiences. Her 2014 *New York Times* bestseller *#GIRLBOSS*, which chronicled her early life as well as her experience as the CEO and founder of fashion empire Nasty Gal, was adapted into a scripted TV series that premiered on Netflix in 2017. Sophia is also the author of *Nasty Galaxy*.

Follow Sophia Amoruso and Girlboss,
and subscribe to the Girlboss newsletter:

Instagram: @SophiaAmoruso
Facebook: Facebook.com/SophiaTheGirlboss
Twitter: @SophiaAmoruso

Instagram: @Girlboss
Facebook: Facebook.com/GirlbossMedia
Twitter: @Girlboss
Newsletter and daily Inspiration: Girlboss.com